The Twelve Deeds

A Brief Life Story of Tonpa Shenrab, the founder of the Bon religion

Translated by Sangye Tandar

Edited by Richard Guard

LIBRARY OF TIBETAN WORKS AND ARCHIVES

ISBN: 81-85102-96-1

Published by the Library of Tibetan Works & Archives and printed at Indraprastha Press (CBT), 4 Bahadurshah Zafar Marg, New Delhi 110002.

Preface

The original Tibetan text from which the present translation is prepared is *sTon pa yang dag rdzogs pa'i sangs rgyas rgyal ba gshen rab mi bo'i mdzad pa bcu gnyis kyi rim pa*, or *mDzad chen bcu gnyis kyi rnam bshad mdor bsdus*, a brief life story of Tonpa Shenrab based on the traditionally known format, the 'twelve deeds'. It was composed in the 1960s by Menri Lopon Sangye Tenzin (d.1977) and was published by The Tibetan Bonpo Foundation in Delhi in 1965. In 1988, the Council for Tibetan Education of His Holiness The Dalai Lama in collaboration with Jadur Sonam Sangpo, the then Bon representative for the Assembly of Tibetan People's Deputies, published this in book form with illustrations, to facilitate the reading material on Bon for Tibetan schoolchildren. It is this later edition on which the present translation is based.

According to the Bon tradition, Tonpa Shenrab was not only the founder of the Bon religion, but also the first Buddha to appear in this 'age of degeneration' (*Kaliyuga*) to save living beings from sufferings. He was believed to have been born 16,016 years[1] ago (B.C.) in the land called Olmo Loongring (*'Ol mo lung ring*),[2] in the innermost part of the Zhang Zhung kingdom then called Tagzing (*sTag gzigs*) and lived 81 *Shen* years,[3] during which he visited Tibet (i.e. Kongpo) once, and taught the people there the basics of Bon practices called 'causal Bon'.

His detailed life story is available in three versions: long, of medium length and short. They are among the class of scriptures which are considered his own 'words' (*mDo*). Therefore, their ultimate source is being traced back to Tonpa Shenrab himself. The long version, *'Dus pa rin po che'i rgyud dri ma med pa gzi brjid rab tu 'bar ba'i mdo* (also called *Dri med gzi brjid* or simply *gZi brjid*),[4] has 61 chapters in 12 volumes. It belongs to the class of scriptures called 'transmission by hearing' (*snyan brgyud*) and was mystically transmitted to Trulku Lodhen Nyingpo (b.1360 A.D.) by Tangchen Mutsa Gyermed, a siddha of the 8th century A.D. Extracts from chapters 7, 8, 9, 10, 11, 12, 13, 14, 15 and 16 of this version have been edited and translated into English by D.L. Snellgrove.[5]

The middle length version, *'Dus pa rin po che'i rgyud gzer mig* (also called *mDo gzer mig* or *gZer mig*),[6] has 18 chapters in two volumes. It belongs to a class of scriptures called 'rediscovered treasure' (*gter ma*) and was rediscovered from Trithang Durtrod (*Khri thang dur khrod*) in Samye by Drangje Tsunpa Sermig. The first seven chapters and part of the eighth of this version have been translated into English by A.H. Francke.[7] The short version, *Dus gsum sangs rgyas byung khungs kyi mdo'*, more popularly known as *mDo 'dus*,[8] has 24 chapters in one volume. It belongs to the same class as *gZer mig* and was rediscovered (in 961 A.D.) in the red stupa (*mChod rten dmar po*) in Samye by two Indian sadhus (*A-tsa-ra mi gnyis*).

The present translation first appeared in *Tibet Journal* (vol. XVII, No.2, 1992). Certain parts of the translation needed correction and retranslation which I did after consulting the original Tibetan text. I wish to thank Vyvyan Cayley, a volunteer editor at LTWA, for proofreading the translation.

Thupten K. Rikey
Research & Translation Bureau (LTWA)

(1) The Deed of Birth
(sku bltams-pa'i mdzad-pa)

gshen-rab spangs-rtogs mthar-phyin bde-bar gshegs//
grangs-med tshogs-bsags grangs-med sgrib-pa sbyangs//
'og-min gnas-su mngon-par sangs-rgyas nas//
'gro-la rnam-brtse-rgyal-bas mi-lus bzhes//
rnam-par bzhes-pa khyed-la phyag-'tshal lo//

I bow to You, Shenrab the Victor,
Who out of compassion for all beings
Manifests in human form.
Having accumulated countless merits and purified countless
    afflictions;
You are enlightened at the abode of the Highest Pure Land;
Your realisation and abandonment are perfect and complete.

Having gone to the south, at the peak of Gongma Zalandare, the capital city of Phagkye *('phags-skyes)*, and meditated upon the five intentions,[9] the Shenrab was born to
his father Mibon Lhabon Gyalbon Thodkar *(mi-bon lha-bon
rgyal-bon thod-dkar)* and mother Machi Lhachi Yochi Gyal
Zhema *(ma-phyi lha-phyi yo-phyi rgyal-bzhad-ma)*, under the
star of Gyal *(rgyal)*, at the time of early dawn, on the 15th
day of the first month *(me-stag-gi zla-ba)* of Spring in the
Wood Male Mouse year. He was born in the royal lineage
of Murig-trul *(dmu-rigs 'phrul)* at the palace of Barpo Sogye
(bar-po so-brgyad), which was the celestial field of Tagzig
Olmo Lungring *(rtag-gzigs 'ol-mo lung-ring)*. In this way,
Shenrab, the wish-fulfilling jewel of three secret types, and
the mandala of the major and minor marks of the enlightened being, came into the world. [From that time] up until

2

Tonpa Shenrab and His two attendants descend from the peak of Gongma Zalandare; He Himself emanated in the form of a cuckoo and His two attendants in the form of two swallows.

Tonpa Shenrab, just born from His mother's right armpit, is being received by the five goddesses in the castle Barpo Sogyed.

the Water Hare year (1963 C.E.), 17,979 years elapsed.

A Brahmin soothsayer named Selkyab Oden (*gsal-khyab 'od-ldan*) examined Him and found the following qualities: the 32 major and 80 minor marks, the 40 root letters and the 108 good aspects of knowledge, an inconceivable mass of rays of light and the 360 aspects of wisdom. This precious being shot forth rays in all directions, and thereupon was named Tonpa Shenrab Mibo-che, the victorious teacher of the teaching of Bon. At the same time, He emanated three members of His retinue and two incarnations. Tonpa Satong Paljor (*ston-pa sa-stong dpal-'byor*) was the teacher before Shenrab. All of His followers were enlightened during His teaching and [at the time of the coming of Shenrab] the teaching had come to an end.

After that, He performed the deeds of youthful play for one year. Then He was enthroned on the seat of the king Murig-trul by the eminent ones of this mundane world. He was offered the mandala of the 3,000 fields of the world and He became the lord of all the entire realms. At that time, the golden rule of the kingdom was offered [to him,] and subsequent to this, the field of craft was introduced among the fields of knowledge, serving as the basis for the teaching of Shenrab.

4

Tonpa Shenrab introduces the nine levels of Bon doctrine and practices.

(2) The Deed of Dissemination
(rnam-par spel-ba'i mdzad-pa)

rgyal-ba'i sras-po dam-pa 'gro-ba'i dpal//
'gro-ba'i ched-bzhes rang-byung sprul-pa'i sku//
'khor-lo bsgyur-rgyal rgyal-po'i gdan-gnon cing//
theg-pa rim-dgus 'gro-ba'i kha-lo bsgyur//
rnam-par spel-ba khyed-la phyag-'tshal lo//

I bow in respect to You, the Disseminator,
The conqueror's son who is the glory of sentient beings;
And who emanated for the welfare of sentient beings,
Who held the throne of universal monarch, and led
Sentient beings through the vehicles' nine stages.[10]

For a period of 12 Shen years, i.e. 1,198 human years, the holders of the nine stages of the vehicle, [who were] His outer, inner and secret retinues, were taught the four causal vehicles, which are the Chashen (*phyva-bshen*), Nangshen (*snang-gshen*), Trulshen ('*phrul-gshen*) and Sishen (*srid-gshen*) of Bon. In addition to this, Genyen (*dge-bsnyen*), Drangsong (*drang-srong*), Akar (*a-dkar*), Yeshen (*ye-gshen*) and the vehicle of Yangtse Lamey (*yang-rtshe bla-med*) were taught. Then at the edifice of Nine Stack Swastika Mountain the Bon was taught to Yulo (*gyu-lo*), Malo (*rma-lo*), Yeshen (*ye-gshen*) and the 360 members of the ocean of Shenrab's [disciples]. In addition, the four doors[11] and the fifth treasure[12] were opened to the followers. Following this, He went to the palace of Wangchen Sadag (*dbang-chen sa-bdag*). On the 15th day of the Water Pig year, the outer, inner and secret Kalachakra [text] having 8,000 chapters was taught. Up to this time, the (second of the) 12 deeds was completed.

Tonpa Shenrab emanates from His body the six divine masters to help the living beings in six realms.

(3) The Deed of Pacifying
(rnam-par dul-ba'i mdzad-pa)

bon-nyid dbyings-nas rang-bzhin lhun-la rdzogs//
sprul-pa'i skyur-bstan 'gro-ba'i don-la dgongs//
tshang-rgyud 'jig-rten bye-ba phrag-brgya na//
'dul-ba'i sprul-sku bye-ba phrag-brgyar 'gyed//
rnam-par 'dul-ba khyed-la phyag-'tshal lo//

I bow to You, the Pacified One.
Bon is naturally and spontaneously complete;
Intending the welfare of sentient beings, it emanated
To the millions of lands of this world
Millions of emanations to pacify them.

Though the mind of the Teacher, with the attributes of the two purities, does not change in terms of time, place or nature, in order to emanate millions of His manifestations He, from the crown of His head down to the heels of His feet, from the major points of His body, from His six consciousnesses, from the pores of His body and from the hairs of His head, emanated the enlightened teachers, such as 33 Dulshen (*'dul-gshen*), Yeshen (*ye-gshen*), Yendul (*gyen-'dul*), the four Shenpos (*gshen-po*), the Shenpos of the four directions and the central, and other millions of emanations into millions of worlds to pacify sentient beings.

Tonpa Shenrab subdues Guling Mati,
Tobu Dodhe, Trishi Wangyal, Dragje Halaratsa
and Guber Gyalpo, who attacked him, having been overwhelmed by aversion, jealousy,
pride and attachment.

(4) The Deed of Leading (Sentient Beings)
(rnam-par 'dren-pa'i mdzad-pa)

gdul-dka' nyon-mongs 'khor-ba'i sems-can la//
mkhyen-dang brtse-ba'i thugs-rjes rab-dgongs shing//
de-nyid sdug-bsngal nyon-mongs zhi-mdzad cing//
ngan-song gnas-spangs thar-pa'i lam-la bkod//
rnam-par 'dren-pa khyed-la phyag-'tshal lo//

I bow in respect to You who,
Being motivated by compassion for the sentient beings
Of this cyclic existence who are difficult to subdue,
Pacified their suffering from afflictions
And released them from the lower realms,
Leading them to the path of liberation.

This worldly realm is tortured by the heavy afflictions of attachment and ignorance. The Shenrab led the following persons of great non-virtue to the state of enlightenment: Trishi Wangyal (*khri-shi dbang-rgyal*), who was overwhelmed by aversion, Dragje Halaratsa (*drag-byed ha-la ra-tsa*), who was overwhelmed by jealousy, Guber Gyalpo (*gu-wer rgyal-po*) who was overwhelmed by pride, Guling Mati ('*gu-ling mati*) who was overwhelmed by desire; and innumerable other sentient beings. In this way, the Shenrab led sentient beings to the state of Buddhahood, the completion of three bodies.

Tonpa Shenrab takes for His consort Hoza
Gyalmed. His other consorts include Poza,
Kongza and the Brahmin girl.

(5) The Deed of Definite (Marriage)
(rnam-par nges-pa'i mdzad-pa)

gang-zhig gang-gis 'dod-pa'i rgya-mtshor byings//
de-nyid de-yi ngang-du bral-ba can//
mi-'bral lha-mo'i ngang-du ro-gcig-pa//
gang-dag mthun-pa mdzad-phyir 'gro-ba'i don//
rnam-par nges-pa khyed-la phyag-'tshal lo//

I bow in respect to You the Definite One,
Who behaves like the beings
Who are drowned in the ocean of suffering;
Yet in reality, You are none other than the deity.

Indra, the king of gods, beseeched the Shenrab to marry (a goddess). However, this was interrupted by a barren lady. In order to show the concordant practice, a marriage was arranged to the 360 ladies (*dpal-'bar*), who are the incarnations of the 360 deities at Rajgirh, and to the princess Hoza Gyalmed-ma (*hos-za rgyal-med-ma*) who is the daughter of Ho Dangwa Yiring (*hos dvangs-ba yig-ring*) and an incarnation of Semo Yumchen Jamma (*sras-mo yum-chen byams-ma*).

12

His son Tobu Bumsang takes birth. He had eight sons, such as Chedbu
Trishe, etc., and two daughters.

(6) The Deed of Emanation
(rnam-par sprul-pa'i mdzad-pa)

rgyal-ba'i sras-po dam-pa 'gro-ba'i dpal//
rabs-chad ma-ning bya-ba'i ngag-gcag phyir//
mi-rje srid-pa 'gro-ba'i don-mdzad-sprul//
rgyal-ba'i sras-po 'gro-ba'i mtha'-ru phyin//
rnam-par sprul-pa khyed-la phyag-'tshal-lo//

I bow to You, the Emanation,
The conqueror's son for the glory of beings,
Who in order to fulfil the wishes of living beings
And to overrule the remarks such as
"Shenrab was impotent or of neutral sex",
Manifested into the king of mankind,
Displayed the worldly life
And completed his mission for the good of others.

Being a fully enlightened one, Tonpa Shenrab does not hold
any worldly lineage. Yet, to continue the royal lineage into
which He manifested and to help other beings, He fathered
the following sons: Tobu Bumsang (*gto-bu 'bum-sangs*),
Chedbu Trishe (*dpyad-bu khri-shes*), Lungden Selva (*lung-
'dren gsal-ba*), Gyundren Dronma (*brgyud-'dren sgron-ma*),
Kong-tsha Wangdhen (*kong-tsha dbang-ldan*), Kongtsha
Trulbu (*kong-tsha 'phrul-bu*), Oldrug Thangpo (*'ol-drug thangpo*) and Dungsob Mucho Demdrug (*gdung-sob ['tshob] mu-cho
ldem-drug*). The daughters born to Him were Shensa
Nechen (*gshen-za ne-chen*) and Shensa Nechung (*gshen-za nechung*).

While they were being born, the following auspicious
signs occurred: the gods of the sky and the nagas of the

earth all assembled; the princesses were showered with ambrosia by the god Brahma and bestowed with the initiation of the wish-fulfilling gem by Indra, the king of gods; Naga Jogpo (*klu'jog-po*) cut their navels with the udumbara flower, and the Naga anand (*klu-dga'-bo*) placed them in Tushita [pure land]; Naga Maldro (*klu mal-dros*) provided the brahmin string through his prayers; the king of marvels added marvels (*phyva*); the king of Mu (*dmu*) tied the string of Mu, and Indra, the king of gods, prayed for their long life. They were examined by the Brahmin's son Gyurba Losal (*'gyur-ba blo-gsal*), and he discovered that they had all the qualities of their father. They appeared to be wrapped in a precious scarf, and were ornamented by the major and minor marks. Very strict with the eight groups of demons, they were very efficient in performing activities for the welfare of sentient beings.

In addition to this, they were very compassionate and intelligent. They understood the import of the Bon religion as soon as their father taught them, and were found to be expert in method as well as patient. In this way the Shenrab's children were emanated for the welfare of sentient beings.

(7) The Deed of Subduing
(rnam-par 'joms-pa'i mdzad-pa)

bon-nyid dbyings-na 'khor-'das dbyer-med cing//
gnyis-med mnyam-pa'i ngang-la gnas-mod-kyang//
m-rtogs-log-pa thugs-rjes 'dul-ba'i phyir//
bstan-pa'i bar-chad nye-bar zhi-bar mdzad//
rnam-par 'joms-pa khyed-la phyag-'tshal-lo//

I bow in respect to You, the Subduer.
Though within the sphere of the nature of Bon
Cyclic existence and nirvana are inseparable,
Yet to pacify misunderstanding and misconception,
Out of compassion You subdued the obstacles to the
teaching.

Though the sphere of the nature of Bon is devoid of adopting and abandoning, and is in a state of non-duality, yet in
terms of conventional Bon, the Pervasive Long-handed
Mara-demon (bdud khyab-pa lag-ring), the son of Mara-
demon Gyalag Thodje (bdud-rgya-lag thod-rje'i bu), who re-
sides at Munpa Zerdan (mun-pa zer-ldan) to the north of
Tsangri (tshangs-ris), saw that his celestial field was to be
emptied by the Shenrab. Therefore, this son displayed nine
miraculous feats to deceive the Teacher Shenrab. His manifestations were in the forms of a god and an acarya, 34
parents, five young men, seven young ladies, seven bro-
thers and eight boys. However, Shenrab recognised them
through His omniscient knowledge, and subdued their feats
through skilful means.

After that, the ninth miraculous manifestation waged
war against Him with millions of soldiers. However, the

Khyabpa, the demon, displays nine different feats and attacks Tonpa Shenrab. Shensa Nechung is rescued from the demons.

entire rain of arrows and weapons had no effect on the
Shenrab. In spite of those, He remained in meditation, in a
state of peace. He replaced the darkness caused by these
Mara-demons with the sun of compassion, and changed
their weapons to lotuses. As a result, faith in Him and His
retinues arose in many of the Mara-demons.

After that, the Mara-demons displayed various feats to
the retinues of the Shenrab such as the city, the castle, the
boy, the girl, the women and so forth. But due to the grace
of the Teacher, they did not become the victims of the
Mara-demons. However, they were able to seduce Shensa
Nechung. She left her native land, Metokling (*me-tog gling*),
and accompanied them into their land of Mara-demons. At
that time Shenrab, who had gone to protect the land of Cha
(*phywa*), was invited back by A-zha (*'A-zha*). In the company
of 5,500 Yungdrung sempas (*g.yung-drung sem-pa*) Shenrab
went to the land of Mara-demons and rescued Shensa Nechung from her seduction by the Mara-demons. Ashamed
of her immoral deeds, she confessed her sin. On their way,
the Shenrab turned the wheel of Dharma, and at this time
the Mara-demon confessed and offered the five forms of
offerings to the Shenrab. Meanwhile, He guided the two
sons of this Mara to the path of liberation.

Again, the Mara-demons displayed the miraculous feat
to steal Shenrab's wealth. Shorba Kyadun (*bdud-phrug shorba rkya-bdun*), the seven children of the Mara-demon, stole
the seven horses of Shen and ran away to Kongpo. As the
Teacher Shenrab sees the appearance of this world like a
purified mirror, he was not attached to the horses; yet seeing that the time was ripe to tame those Tibetan people
who were of the race of demons and to conquer the Maras,
He went after the horses. Meanwhile, the Maras emanated

various scenes such as filling the whole country with flames, stopping the waters of the oceans and blocking the roads by storms and heavy snowfalls. All of these were pacified by the great compassionate one. For the welfare of sentient beings in the future, He destroyed the mountain belonging to the Mara-demons and emanated from His heart the great Bon mountain to replace it.

After that, the Mara-demons again waged war; however, this time the Shenrab subdued them by summoning in the sky the soldiers of the protector deity Dralha (*dgra-lha*), and transforming their arrows and poison into beautiful flowers. In this way, the forces of the Mara-demons lost the battle against the Shenrab. As a result, great faith in the Shenrab instantly arose in the parents of Pervasive Mara-demon, Kongje Karpo, the then chieftain of Kongpo principalities, and the people of Kongpo, who had previously taken the side of the Mara-demon. They confessed their sins and returned the seven horses. Kongje Karpo offered Him his daughter, Kongtsa Tricham (*kong-za khri-lcam*), for His consort. Finally they all became His followers and were enlightened through His teachings. Seeing this, Pervasive Mara-demon challenged the spiritual power of Shenrab and performed the miraculous feats of [manifesting] ladies, a precious treasury, a lotus tree and medicinal plants, but was defeated. Again, out of jealousy, he set fire to the treasury of scriptures (*gto yi bka' sgrom*), but the great compassion and prayers of Shenrab transformed the flames and smokes into 100,000 Shenrabs for the benefit of others. The five seed letters called the 'five letters of great valour' (*dpa' bo 'bru lnga*) were procured from the burning treasury and 368 letters were developed from them. In this way, the teachings of Shenrab were disseminated far and wide.

(8) The Deed of Victory
(rnam-par rgyal-ba'i mdzad-pa)

ston-pa rnam-mkhyen dpal-gyi sgron-me'i-mchog//
bon-nyid dbyings-su mya-ngan 'das-mod-kyang//
thugs-rje rgyun-mi 'chad-par gnas-pa'i phyir//
bstan-pa rnam-gsum rjes-su bzhag-par mdzad//
rnam-par rgyal-ba khyed-la phyag-'tshal-lo//

I bow in respect to You, the Victor,
Whose omniscient knowledge is the excellent light of glory.
Although You are now no more in this world
As you have entered the state of suchness,
Yet to bestow the stream of compassion
You left this world the three aspects of the teaching.

As for His deeds of victory: the Shenrab entrusted to the
then universal kings the holy objects that symbolised His
mind and body and the voluminous teachings of sutra and
tantra to symbolise His speech. From among those universal kings, Gya Kongtse Trulgyi Gyalpo (*Gya kong-rtse 'phrul-*
gyi rgyal-po), the reincarnation of King Selchog Dampa (*gsal-*
mchog dam-pa), was born to father Kadhala Sergyi Dogchen
(*ka-dha-la gser-gyi mdog-can*) and mother Mutri Sel-Odma
(*mu-khri gsal-'od-ma*) at Gyalag Odme'i-ling (*rgya-lag 'od-ma'i*
gling) in the palace of Trigo Tsegya (*khri-sgo rtse-brgya*), in
the centre of the city of Trulgyur Kodpa ('*phrul-bsgyur bkod-*
pa). This boy was examined by a soothsayer, who found in
him all the good marks of a great man. Therefore, he was
named Gya Kongtse Trulgyi Gyalpo. When the boy was
nine years old, he prostrated and prayed to the Shenrab.
Very soon he had a vision and attainment on the 25th of

Tonpa Shenrab entrusts the three aspects of His teachings to Kongtse Trulgyal.

the month. After that, he conceived the idea of constructing a big temple (*gsas-khang*) in the Lake Mu-khyu-dal (*mu-khyud gdal*) as a means to accumulate merits for his next life.

After having subdued the hundreds of demons, he laid the foundation and it reached above the surface of the sea on the 15th day. However, his parents failed to keep it secret, and therefore the demons ran away. The boy was very discouraged because of this and roamed here and there. Meanwhile, due to the power of his previous prayers, he met Chasey Kengtse Lanme (*phya-sras keng-tse lan-med*). The Kengtse asked the boy questions and raised some doubts [in the boy's mind]. At last he realised that Kengtse was a Yungdrung sempa. The boy begged his pardon, with confession and contrition. The Kengtse assembled all the gods and nagas, and completed the construction of the temple, [complete] with statues. It was then named Self-illuminated Temple on the Sea (*dkar-nag bkra-gsal rgya-mtsho'i gling-thog-'bar*). When demons once again attempted to damage the temple, the Kengtse invoked the Shenrab's help. Then the omniscient Shenrab, with His entire retinue of 5,500 Yungdrung sempas, flew into the sky with a miraculous display of power and pacified the manifestations of the demons. Then, in collaboration with Sridpa Sangpo Bumtri, the principal omniscient being of methods, the Shenrab taught His followers in detail the Bon classified into five categories, the 'four doors' and the 'treasury' as fifth. He inaugurated the temple and consecrated the holy objects in there in a most elaborate manner. In this way, He led sentient beings, by way of various analogies and methods.

Tonpa Shenrab renounces the worldly life and becomes a monk.

Tonpa Shenrab leads the ascetic life.

(9) The Deed of Knowledge
(rnam-par rig-pa'i mdzad-pa)

'di-ltar snang-ba 'jig-rten g.yeng-ba'i tshogs//
skad-cig rmi-lam sgyu-ma lta-bur gzigs//
ma-dag sdug-bsngal 'khor-ba bsgral-ba'i phyir//
dag-pa rnam-ldan khyim-spangs rab-tu-byung//
rnam-par rig-pa khyed-la phyag-;tshal-lo//

I bow in respect to You, the Knowledgeable,
Who saw the appearance of this world as
Momentary like a dream, and like a magical performance.
In order to liberate beings from the suffering of cyclic existence,
You left behind the worldly life and joined the ascetic life of pure morality.

The Teacher Shenrab, the compassionate one having skilful means, by His omniscient knowledge saw the four rivers of the sufferings of birth, aging, sickness and death, in the four directions of the Palace Trimon Gyal Zhed (*gsas-mkhar khri-smon rgyal-bzhad*). This persuaded Him to develop the thought definitely to leave cyclic existence. Then, on the 3,100th human or 31st Shen year, when He was about to become a monk, different reactions of happiness and sorrow came from different sentient beings. Yikyi Khyichung (*yid-kyi khye'u-chung*) and many others who had not completed their learning were very happy. However, women with a coarse attachment cried; the Pervasive Mara-demon and his retinues were delighted. Then the Shenrab, with the intention of destroying the Mara-demon of pride and ending His aggregates, went to the place where the White Stupa of

Purity was located and, renouncing the householder's life, became a monk.

To begin with, He gave up His outer ornaments such as His bracelets and clothes. Then He cut His hair and so forth, and then lived on alms for His livelihood. Leaving behind His retinue and kingdom, He went to Metokling to lead an ascetic life. Non-devoted members of His retinue such as Shenbu Kongtsha dissuaded the devoted members from renouncing their homes. Touching His feet, all of these requested Him not to leave them, but He did not listen to them. Then He was again requested to stay at the top of the palace, and was offered various meals on golden and silver plates; still He did not agree to accept the food. Then, forsaking His home, palace, property, queen, son, and disciples, He went off alone and slept on the ground, using bark for His bedsheet. The next morning, when the sun rose, He recited the names of the thousand Buddhas. At dawn, He circumambulated the Shambo Lhatse and recited the names of the gods and the Shen. When the sun rose, He washed and cleansed His body and then recited the root mantras. Next He engaged in restricting the foods He was taking. He took the three types of white food such as milk, curd and butter, and refrained from meat, garlic, wine and so forth. After that, He donned monk's robes and shook His body, whereupon wings developed from His body and He transformed into a Shang-shang bird. In spite of the request of His retinue, He flew into the empty sky and approaching Drangsrong Legdhan (*drang-srong legs-ldan*) in the Highest Pure Land, He received the teaching on the rules of monk-hood. Then He descended to the Thirty-third Heaven where He lived an ascetic life for one year and turned the wheel of Bon. After that He did the ascetic practice following the lifestyle of monkeys for one year in the Land of the Four Great Kings, where again He turned the wheel of Bon. Then at Metokling which was at the border of Olmo Lung-ring, He did the ascetic practice following the lifestyle of birds during the day and of human beings in the night for one year. The Pervasive Mara-demon and his countless retinue developed faith in Him, and therefore He turned the wheel of Bon for them. In this way, He did the three types of ascetic practices for three Shen years in order to set an example for all unenlightened living beings. Then at the dusk of the day that concluded His ascetic practices He subdued the Maras, in the middle of the night while seated in meditative equipoise, and in the early dawn was fully enlightened. At that time, there was no division in the retinue and, therefore, headed by Yikyi Khyichung, everyone gathered around the Teacher like a gathering of clouds.

Here the Teacher taught them the four words of the wheel of Bon. Everyone obeyed with faith and devotion. The retinue was classified into four groups (*sde-bzhi*) and eight individuals (*ya-brgyad*). Yikyi Khyichung became the abbot and the Teacher acted as the preceptor and bestowed the ordination. Males lined up on the right and females on the left. Thereupon, He taught the basic and additional vows of the orders of an overnight ordination, layman ordination, novice ordination, full ordination and so forth. He explained in detail the division and the classification of the precepts. In this way, He enlightened His followers with the teachings on pure morality and enabled them to bring an end to their samsaric life.

Tonpa Shenrab teaches the Bon of three levels to suit the
three different mental dispositions of living beings—
sharp, mediocre and dull.

(10) The Deed of Solitude
(rnam-par dben-pa'i mdzad-pa)

gang-dag 'jig-rten g.yeng-bar gyur-pa'i tshogs//
de-nyid sdug-bsngal rnam-par dben-pa'i phyir//
g.yeng-ba'i tshogs-spangs 'khor-spangs dgon-pa-mdzad//
gcig-pur-mi-yengs bon-nyid don-la-bsgoms//
rnam-par dben-pa khyed-la phyag-'tshag-lo//

I bow in respect to You, the Solitary One,
Who wishes to remove the sufferings which are caused by
The collections of the worldly scattering (of mind).
You abandoned all the accumulations of scattering and
   cyclic existence,
In the solitary place where You meditated in isolation on
   the nature of Bon.

The Teacher sat in isolation from others at the Nine Stack
Swastika Mountain in a forest. There He remained in perfect silence. The followers of the Teacher gathered around
Him like a gathering of clouds. These followers were classified into two groups. The ones with the brighter intellect
such as Tsunpa Khyabpa (*btsun-pa khyab-pa*), Tobu Bumsang
(*gto-bu 'bum-sangs*) and so forth were taught the instructions
for achieving enlightenment within one lifetime. He instructed them in the 'ultimate point' and 'primordial basis'. To
delineate the above meaning, the analogy is given of the
rising sun dispelling darkness simultaneously in all parts of
the world. In this way, the definite meaning is simultaneously shown, whereby wisdom is accomplished. However,
for ones with lesser intellect such as Shensa and others, He
generated the knowledge of wisdom in them. He instructed

them in the gradual path of spiritual practices, such as the
path to be reborn in god and human realms, the gradual
eradication of the afflictive emotions in the nine lower
stages and the obscuration of wisdom in the 13 higher
stages, in the manner in which the moon gradually in-
creases from new to full. Then He instructed them to build
their retreat cells in isolation in deep forest, on islands, in
cremation grounds or caves and to meditate unaccompanied
by other people, like an injured deer abandoned by the
flock.

(11) The Deed of Liberation
(rnam-par grol-ba'i mdzad-pa)

rgyal-ba'i sras-po dam-pa mthar-phyin-cing//
dka'-ba rnam-spyod sbyangs-thob mi-mnga'-yang//
'gro-ba'i don-dgongs sbyangs-thob mthar-phyin-cing//
mthar-phyin dga'-ba bde-ldan mdzad-pa rdzogs//
rnam-par grol-ba khyed-la phyag-'tshal-lo//

I bow in respect to You, the liberated one,
Who has perfected the practice of Yungdrung sempa.
Though You did not need to follow the ascetic practice of
   learning,
Yet to show the followers how You have gone and what
   they should follow,
You have shown the deeds of happiness and bliss.

Then He taught His followers that in order to practise the
realisation of the view, one should look at it from the
highest to the lowest, and for the practice of behaviour, one
should climb from the bottom to the top. Their basis should
be great compassion and their means should be the 10 per-
fections. In this way, the order of the stages is shown. In
order to meditate on the highest stage of the great vehicle,
the nature of Bon and the realisation of Bon are released in
the sphere of one moment. The environment and the beings
therein are inseparable. Cyclic existence and the state of
liberation are also inseparable. In addition to this, He
[showed] the perfection of adopting and abandoning. The
door of the vehicle is not blocked and the sport of the practice is realised. The nature of Bon is perfected and the mind
is in the centre of bliss. He established the characteristics of

Tonpa Shenrab teaches the Bon of nine stages and entrusts them to the respective disciples.

the time, the non-time, the past, the present and the future. After that He showed the formation of the aeon, the teaching of Bon in the future, the history of the marks and qualities, and the attainments of the state of Bon. The followers to whom they were shown were: the millions of the outer retinue, the millions of the intermediate retinue, the 1,600 of the inner retinue, the 3,500 of the secret retinue, the 5,500 Yungdrung sempas who formed the personal retinue, the 360 Yeshen, the eight incarnate Yungdrung sempas and the beings of this mundane world. In order to accomplish the welfare of the beings of the future, He passed the inexpressible Bon to them.

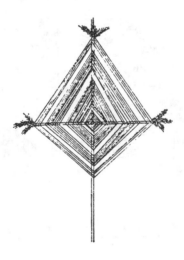

32

Shenrab entering into the state of mahaparinirvana.

(12) The Deed of Accomplishment
(Passing Beyond Sorrow)
(rnam-par grub-pa'i mdzad-pa)

rgyal-ba'i sku-la skye-'chi mi-mnga'-yang//
bon-can mtshan-ma mi-rtag dper-bstan-phyir//
bon-nyid dbyings-su mya-ngan 'da'-tshul-bstan//
mkha'-mnyam klong-bdal bon-nyid dbyings-su-'khod//
rnam-par grub-pa khyed-la phyag-'tshal-lo//

I bow in respect to You, the Accomplished One.
Although You are beyond the bonds of birth and death,
Yet to show the analogy of impermanence with respect to
   conventional Bon,
You showed the mode of passing beyond sorrow of the
   sphere of Bon
And arrayed the sphere of the essence of Bon as vast as the
   sky.

The stanzas in praise of the teacher Shenrab by A-zha
Sangba Dhodu ('A-zha gsang-ba mdo-sdud) say:

The nature of Bon has neither birth nor death.
The nature of mind is primordially devoid of the Mara-
   demon of death.
Similarly, though Shenrab has neither birth nor death,
Yet to tame impermanent beings,
And to show the helplessness of this life,
He showed the passing beyond sorrow of this abode of
   cyclic existence.

At first, when He was at the Nine Stack Swastika Mountain, He manifested a magical body from His mouth, so that the cause of sickness surrounded His body, and it in turn bound His consciousness. Gradually the suffering of birth and aging came to Him. Then He said, "At this time, my four aggregates are attacked by the diseases which are the factors of disintegration and therefore my life is in danger." The members of the retinue were very worried and invited Him to come from the forest. He was requested to stay in the palace of Trimon Gyalshed (*khri-smon rgyal-bzhad*). Tobu did a mystical treatment and Chebu (*dpyad-bu*) performed an operation. Therefore, in order to show the validity of conventional truth, He recovered from the ailment and felt very comfortable. After some time, again He caused the ailment to worsen. This time Yikyi Khyichung, Malo and Yulo beseeched Him not to pass beyond sorrow. At the time of passing beyond sorrow, He spoke His will and the Instruction of Liberation with Ease at Death.

At dusk, at the abode of Trimon Gyalshed, He subdued the millions of the forces of Mara. At the Nine Stack Swastika Mountain, in the 82nd Shen year or 8200th human year, in the first winter month of the Water Hare year, He passed beyond sorrow with all the many millions of good omens. The members became divided (over the distribution of relics) and they sent for the Tsunpa Khyabpa to invite 'A-zha. However, 'A-zha experienced the presence of a live Teacher and offered various types of offerings to Him. As the Shenrab, the father of sentient beings had passed away, sentient beings were overwhelmed by anxiety and sorrow. Since He was no longer in this world, they could not show Him to others, and therefore all the ritual and ceremonies were performed as a fulfilment of homage. The four groups of His retinue and the eight individuals had a discussion, and then placed the relics in a golden tomb. In order to provide for all equally, they searched through the body ashes and offered various offerings in accordance with the ritual text of 18 chapters (*cho-ga 'phrin-las bco-brgyad*). After the cremation the relics were divided among the humans, gods and nagas as their object of refuge.

The next year, in the Wood Male Dragon year, from among the countless members of Shen, the assembly of 13 Yungdrung sempas compiled the Shenrab Teachings. From the passing beyond sorrow of the Shenrab up until the Water Hare year, 1,800 human years were completed and this ended the 'body doctrine' (*sku-bstan*) period. After that year, the Water Dragon, in the last month of Autumn, His successor Mucho Demdrug with all his retinues from heaven came to the place where the four self-born stupas were located and this began the 'speech doctrine' (*gsung bstan*) period. From that time up until now, 7,979 human years have passed. Mucho turned the wheel of Bon for a period of three Shen years. Many eminent scholars appeared at that time. The most excellent ones among them were Trithog Partsa (*khri-thog spar-tsa*), Mutsa Trahe (*dmu-tsa tra-he*) and Huli Parya (*hu-li spar-ya*) of Tagzig, Lhadag Ngagdol (*lha-bdag sngags-grol*) of India, Legtang Mangpo (*legs-tang rmang-po*) of China and Ser-thog Chejam (*gser-thog lce-'byams*) of Tromshen (*khrom-gshen*). They were called the six scholars who were the ornaments of the world. Countless other scholars propagated the teaching of Shenrab throughout the Land of Tibet, Zhang zhung and China. Thus ends the brief explanation of the 12 deeds of the Buddha Shenrab.

Notes

1. This calculation and other dates are based on *Sangs rgyas kyi bstan rtsis nor bu'i phreng ba zhes bya ba* (composed in 1842) by Abbot Nyima Tenzin (b.1813).
2. This land has not yet been able to be identified on the modern world map.
3. According to the Bon belief, one *Shen* year is equal to one hundred calendrical years known to human beings—"human year". Calculated in this manner, Tonpa Shenrab lived 8,100 years.
4. Published by The Tibetan Bonpo Foundation, Delhi 1967-69.
5. *The Nine Ways of Bon*, London Oriental Series, vol. 18, London 1976; reprint by Prajna Press, Boulder 1980.
6. Published by The Tibetan Bonpo Foundation, Delhi 1965.
7. "A Book of the Tibetan Bonpos", *Asia Major*, Leipzig 1924, 1926, 1927, 1930; *Asia Major* (News Series) 1, London 1949.
8. Published recently for the first time outside Tibet by Khedup Gyatsho, Bonpo Monastic Centre, Dholanji, Oachghat, Via Solan, H.P. India.
9. The five intentions are: the intention to take birth at a particular place, to take birth in a particular world, to take birth in a particular country, to take birth in a particular caste, and to take birth in the womb of a particular woman.
10. *theg-pa rim-pa dgu: phyva-gshen theg-pa, snang-gshen theg-pa, 'phrul-gshen theg-pa, srid-gshen theg-pa, dge-bsnyen theg-pa, drang-srong theg-pa, a-dkar theg-pa, ye-gshen theg-pa* and *bla-med theg-pa.*
11. *chab-dkar, chab-nag, 'phan-yul* and *dpon-gsas.*
12. *mtho-thog.*